JN409432

SENSE OF AROMA

인쇄 2010년 3월 31일
발행 2010년 4월 5일

지은이 | 한신디아 외 30명
펴낸이 | 임수홍
발행처 | 도서출판 국보
등록 | 제 324-2006-0023호
주소 | 서울시 강동구 길동 395-3 2층
전화 | 02-476-2757 / 476-7260
전송 | 02-476-2759
이메일 | kbmh11@hanmail.net
홈페이지 | http://cafe.daum.net/lsh19577

값 19,800원
ISBN 978-89-93533-10-1

Translated By Cynthia Han
And Her Companions

KOOKBO Publishing Company

Translated By Cynthia Han
And Her Companions

여기에 실린 글들은
애틀랜타-중앙일보
시카고-중앙일보
W's잡지
뉴욕-한국일보
서울-한국문학신문 등에 발표한 사진과 시 모음집입니다.

This complete book of pictures
and poems were published in:

[뉴욕/한국일보]
NEW YORK-KOREA TIMES

[시카고/중앙일보]
CHICAGO-KOREA DAILY

[USA/우먼잡지W's]
USA-W's MAGAZINE

[애틀랜타/중앙일보]
ATLANTA-KOREA DAILY

[서울/한국문학신문]
SEOUL-KOREA LITERATURE NEWSPAPER

Cynthia Han (Poetess)

Born in Gyeongju, South Korea.
Graduated from College with a music major and became an Assistant Professor for a while.
Since 2002, I have volunteered as a translator for Ulsan Metropolitan City.
In 2009, I debuted as a poet and received an award for my poem entitled 'Life.'
My work has appeared in many major Newspapers and books.

Email: eshan0661@hanmail.net

Yoan Yun (Photographer)

Born in 1960 in South Korea. Immigrated to USA in 1976. Attended and studied fine art and photography at the School of Visual Arts.

Graduated with a Bachelor's Degree in Fine Arts.

I am an abstract post impressionist artist and had many fine art exhibitions. Since 2007, I have had an interest in photography and have had two photography exhibitions and pictures appearing in a few newspaper articles weekly. I hope everyone enjoys this book and many books to follow.

Jacqueline Pynn (Assistant)

She was born in New York. At 14 moved to Dunwoody,
Georgia where she graduated from high school
and went to work.
After working for nine years.
She decided to become an RN graduating from
The Nell Hodgson Woodruff School of Nursing at Emory
University with a BSN.
She has had a full career working with cancer patients,
now working as an Oncology Case Manager.
She loves the outdoors, photography, music and poetry.
One thing she has learned from working with the chronically
ill is to live life to its fullest and to always be happy.
She has enjoyed translating poetry and appreciates
the chance she has been given.

Joan Ballenger (Assistant)

Joan is from the United States of America and is currently living in Ulsan, South Korea.

She was educated at National Louis University in Chicago where she holds a bachelor's degree in Business Management.

She went on to Webster University where she pursued a Master of Arts Degree in Business Management.

She is currently working at SDA language Institute as an English teacher.

Joan enjoys travelling and volunteering with many non profits organization.

She always enjoys translating wonderful poetry by Cynthia Han.

Lucy Yoon (Assistant)

Lucy was born in Korea.
She emigrated to the United States
when she was nine years old.
Lucy grew up in New York and graduated
with a bachelor's degree in English Literature.
She's had many adventures traveling all over the world.
She played many different sports.
Today she works with software developers
as a project manager.

[The Beginning]

The Beginning

Climb to the mountain summit
To greet the first sunrise on the first day of New Year

Those who begin the day cherishing a dream
Shall not fear the new life ahead

When the mind is calmed from chaos
The heart can be filled with many dreams

Release those dreams toward the rising red sun
Be blessed with a healthy, loving and joyful New Year!

Cynthia Han

[KOREA LITERATURE NEWSPAPER 01. 01. 2010]

Thirty Exquisite Poets Chosen
by Yoan Yun and Cynthia Han

Sense of Aroma

Table of Contents

1. Cynthia Han
- –Sea Fog
- –Life

2. Jong Hwan An
- –Enticing
- –Poetry Writing

3. Seon Yeong Moon
- –Winter Fog

4. Beom Soon Hwang
- –Symbol Study

5. Jong Rae Park
- –Fallen Leaf

6. Mi Ya Jeon
- –Perfume
- –Memory of My Hometown

7. So Yeong Seo

−Adonis Amurensis

−Buddha's Birthday

8. Ok Soon Kim

−Chance Encounter

9. Gyeong Hi Lee

−The Phantom of the Opera

10. Soo Il Kim

−Hey

11. Ji Seon Mo

−The Grandpa Next Door

12. Tae Yeong Yang

−Nostalgia

13. Geum Ju Jo

−Evening Twilight

−Rainy Day

14. Ki Ye Jeon

−The Deep Breath of the Female Diver

−Pouring Rain

15. Jong Eun Im

–Standing on a Snowfield

–Marching in the Midsummer

16. Woo Chang Lee

–Winter Letter

17. Jeong Chae Jeong

–Grandma's Childhood

18. In Sook Park

–Spring

–What Should We Do

19. Yeong Jun Yu

–Farmer's Market in the Afternoon

20. Sa Ik Jang

–Strolling

21. Chong Kyu Park

–Baekdu and Chunji!

–Do So

22. Yong Bok Kim

–Letter

–Being in Love

23. In Soo Kim

–Seogwipo

24. Blasio Kim

–Mother

–Eternal Island, Dokdo

25. Seon Mi Jo

–Love

26. Seung Seok Han

–Because You're Coming

27. Cheon Do Hwa

–Hopeless One

–The Wind Cries in Hiding

28. Gil Ok Lee

–The Cactus

–Someone Who Loves Me

29. Jeong Deok Kim

–When Do You Come Back Again

–A Wish for Unification of Korea

30. Sang Byeong Cheon

–Going Back to Heaven

인생

한신디아

어느 날 가던 길을 멈추고 뒤를 돌아본다

같이 걸어가겠다던 친구들이 있었는데
잘나고 이기적인 충고로 그들을 쫓아버렸다

죽을 때까지 함께하자던 연인이 있었는데
나약한 질투로 그 사람을 떠나게 했다

꽃을 들고 몰려온 존경의 눈들이 있었는데
고지식한 설교로 그들의 귀를 막게 했다

삭막한 인생길을 걸으며 뒤를 돌아보니
그리움으로 패인 발자국만 나를 따르고 있다.

Life

Cynthia Han

One day I stopped along my path looking back

There were friends who wished to accompany me
Boastful and selfish advice turned them away

There was a lover devoted to be together until death
Insecure jealousy made him leave

There were swarming respectful eyes with flowers
Blocking their ears with simple-minded lectures

While passing down this dreary life's road in retrospect
Only footprints deepened by yearning were following me.

[ATLANTA-KOREA DAILY]

[Life]

[Sea Fog]

신마

한신디아

어둑새벽 동해에 안개가 피어나면
고기잡이하는 마음은 엄숙에 가깝다

소름끼치는 기운으로 실갯대를 저으면
거무스레한 바다는 수마처럼 일렁인다

그물이 손에서 빠르게 미끄러져 나갈 땐
물속을 떠도는 절규들이 깨어나지 않도록
걸려드는 파도를 소리없이 넘어야 한다

전해오는 주문으로 단을 맞추어 주고
해가 뜨는 열 빛으로 신마가 물러나면

발밑의 어두운 서룬 파도는
푸른 희망으로 잔잔히 다시 살아나
차갑지만 다행한 숨으로 만선을 허락한다.

Sea Fog

Cynthia Han

Early dawn fog is swelling on the East Sea
Fishing heart is closer to divine

When gooseflesh vitality rows the oar
Darkened sea is swayed like a seahorse

When the fishing net slides out of the hand
The wandering bellowing in the water not to be awakened
Cross over the soundless waves that are caught

Giving an order melodiously hypnotizing
Sea fog is drawn by the bouyant light of the rising sun

Shadowy anguished wave underfoot
Gracefully alive again with refreshing aspiration
With chill but a grateful breath allow abundance.

[CHICAGO-KOREA DAILY]

미련2

안종환

잠자는 수첩 속에
수줍은 듯
다소곳이 숨어 있는 전화번호 하나

세월이 겹치고 넘어지는 동안
서걱거리는 억새 말조차
단 한 번 오간 적 없지만

행여나 하는 마음에
수첩을 바꿀 때마다
차마
버리질 못하고 또 옮겨 적는다.

Enticing

Jong Hwan An

In the sleeping address book
Bashfully
A phone number hides

While time is piled and tumbled
A grappling pampas grass conversation
We never had before

Heavy desire to receive that call
Couldn't read it
Therefore the address book is revised.

[CHICAGO-KOREA DAILY]

[Enticing]

시를 쓰다

안종환

불현듯, 섬광처럼 빛나는
작은 씨앗들이 생각을 물고 춤을 춘다
자리를 박차고 일어나
빠른 손놀림으로 하나씩 쓰다듬기 시작한다
자세히 살펴보니 썩 잘 생긴 놈이 아니다

허탈한 심정으로 밤길을 헤맨다
잡힐 듯 잡히지 않는 침묵을 좇아
온 우주를 헤집다가
무념의 나락으로 떨어진다
답답함이 절망의 옷을 입고 나를 짓누른다

생각을 놓아버리고
고요의 언덕에 몸을 누인다
작은 새싹들이 꼬물꼬물 움을 트더니
서로 부딪히고 넘어졌다 일어서기를 거듭하며
이리 꾸불, 저리 꾸불 줄 서기를 시작한다

죽음보다 힘겨운 이 산고(産苦)
연애하는 듯 달콤한 괴로움이여.

Poetry Writing

Jong Hwan An

Suddenly, like a bolt of flash
Tiny seeds are dancing in thought
They stand from their place
One by one begins the quick handed stroking
After careful observation they are not so attractive

Wandering around in the dark streets with a feeling of emptiness
Chasing a silence that seems obtainable but cannot be caught
Digging around the entire universe
Then falling into hell
The crushing frustration dressed in despair

Letting go of these feelings
Lay the body on a hill of silence
Small blossoming buds wiggle their way out
They collide against each other repeatedly falling and standing
Bending this way, bending that way they begin to stand in a line

The labor is more difficult than death
Sweet sorrow is like a relationship.

[NEW YORK-KOREA TIMES]

겨울안개

문선영

새벽 미명 저만큼
하얀 버선발로 살포시 내려앉은 은빛날개
떨고 섰는 여린 가지를 품는다

산허리 돌고 돌 담장 돌아
아련한 그리움으로 다가선 솜사탕
어머니 품속처럼 아늑한데
찬바람 시새워 가시 세우고 살갗을 파고든다

다가서면 멀어지고 멀어지면 다가서는
보이느니 잡히지 않는 애절함

가녀린 가지마다 그리움 서리꽃으로 남기고
마중나온 아침 햇살에 환한 미소로 자리를 내어주곤
유유히 떠나가는 온유한 당신.

Winter Fog

Seon Yeong Moon

Over the dawn
Silver wing set softly with white socked foot
Embracing a tree branch that stands shaking

Turn around the hillside turn around the stone wall
Cotton candy comes closer with heart-broken desire
Snug like mother's arm
Cut into the flesh as the edge of the thorn, with envy of the wind

Drift apart when getting closer getting closer when drifts apart
Can see it but can not be caught, bitterness

The yearning frosty flower remains on every pitiful branch
Giving up the seat when receiving the morning sun light with a bright smile
Then you who is gentle, leaves freely.

[ATLANTA-KOREA DAILY]

[Winter Fog]

[Symbol Study]

기호공부

황범순

오늘 하루도 참 바빴습니다
많은 사람과 많은 얘기도 나누었습니다
돌아오는 길엔 소낙비도 한줄기 시원스레 내려주었습니다
그런데 오늘 밤 왜 이리도 외롭고 허전할까요
꼭 혼자 버려진 느낌입니다

낡은 연립 옥상 장독대 옆에
! 하나로 서 있습니다
? 하나로 서 있는 지도 모릅니다
, ... : 잠시 그런 걸까요
– ~ “ ”/ ”( ) 잠시 이런 걸까요

지구본을 돌리듯 찬찬히 한 바퀴 둘러보아도
불빛 따스한 온기들은 저희들끼리만 낄낄거리고
난
낡은 연립 검은 옥상 위에서
팔을 휘젓다가 목을 돌리다가
버리는 발자국만 자꾸 따라 밟고 있습니다.

Symbol Study

Beom Soon Hwang

It was busy today
I had many conversation with an acquaintance
Refreshing rain poured on the way home
But why am I lonely and depressed tonight
I feel like I am deserted

At the top of an old apartment building
! Stand up as one
? Stand up as one
, ... :Standing up as one temporarily
– ~ “ ”/ ”( ) Only temporarily doing this as one

Look around slowly like turning a sphere
The lights are giggling amongst themselves
But I’m
On the top of the old dark apartment building
Swinging my arms and circling my neck
Continuously occupying the abandoned foot prints.

[NEW YORK–KOREA TIMES]

낙엽

박종래

어제까지
푸른 떡을 빚어
바람의 꿀물 발라
나누어 주었네

지금은
퇴색된 삼베옷 갈아입고
바람 빗자루가 스쳐간 모서리에
개떡처럼 켜켜이 누워
제 몸을 삭히고 있구나

뼈아픈 이별을 모아
스스로 한없이 낮아진
동면의 담요 속에
겉 속 썩음 참아내는
미래가 잉태될 정액알갱이
행여 다람쥐 올까 봐
꼭꼭 숨어 있어라

지나던 까치도 두리번거리다
목화송이 발자국만 남기고 간다.

Fallen Leaf

Jong Rae Park

Until yesterday
A rice cake was made
Pasted with liquid honey of wind
Was distributed

Now
Changing into worn out linen clothes
At the edge where the wind broom scud
Lying like overlapped tasteless sliced bread
Digesting its own body

Gathering the bone crushingly painful breakups
Endlessly lowered itself
Inside the hibernating blanket
Enduring the rotting from the inside and out
Grains of semen that impregnate the future
Are hiding deep inside
In case a squirrel came along

Even the magpie that used to come around
Goes and leaves behind only a cluster of footprints.

[NEW YORK-KOREA TIMES]

[Fallen Leaf]

향수(香水)

전미야

향수(香水)
목선에 살짝 품으면
달짝지근한 시원함이
봄바람처럼 안긴다

은은한 향은
여성스러움을 돋보이게 하고

몽환적인 신비감을 주는
가장 비싼 물로 만들어진 향은
이내 날아가 버리지만

가슴이 만든
사람 내음은
사랑의 향기로
닫힌 마음 열어

깊은 산골 맑음으로
메마른 가슴을 흥건히 적시어

싱그런 웃음
꿈틀거리게 하는
고귀한 향(香)이다.

Perfume

Mi Ya Jeon

Perfume
Spray a little on the neckline
Sweet aroma is
Lain like a spring breeze

Discreet incense
The woman's charisma elevating

Contains a meditative mystical affection
Made with the most exquisite liquid
Even though it evaporates swiftly

Pouring devotion and soul into
Opening the human mind
With fragrances of love
That heals many hearts

Sodden meager hearts
With the translucent depth of the valley

Sweet smile
Atingle with
Noble incense.

[W's Magazine USA]

정든 내고향

전미야

추운 겨울이면
가족끼리 둘러앉아
어머니 정 나누던 내 고향

밤이면 호롱불 밝혀
코밑은 굴뚝 되어
오소리 굴 같이
즐거웠던 그 시절

햇살 따사로운 날이면
옹기종기 앉아
찐 고구마에
동치미 국 마시던 그 옛날

너무나 멀리 와 버린 지금
추억 되뇌며 그리워하지만
세월은 주름살에 들어 앉아
외로운 섬이 된다.

Memory of My Hometown

Mi Ya Jeon

During the cold winter days
Surrounded by close family
Sharing mother's love in my hometown

The oil lamp lit at night causing
Bottom of nose to become like a chimney
Like a badger's cave
Those were happy days

On a bright sunny day
Family sitting closely
Eating steamed sweet potatoes
And drinking kimchee soup, good old days

Now, living so far away
Yearning for old memories
Memories are engraved on the wrinkles
I become a solitude island.

[NEW YORK-KOREA TIMES]

[Buddha's Birthday]

부처님 오신 날

서소영

수종사 앞마당엔
벚나무 꽃잎이 툭 툭 떨어져
주단을 깔아 놓고
오가는 손님을 반긴다

그 누가 쌓아 올린 돌탑일까
돌들마다 얹혀진 소망의 무게
이 화사한 봄날 무겁게 느껴진다

연등을 매다는 손길마다
정성이 가득하고
형형색색 불 밝힌 연등엔
삼라만상 인연의 실타래
윤회의 긴 터널을 지나간다

헛된 욕망 끌어안고
소유하기 위해 혼탁해진 마음
스스로 뼈를 깎는 수행승 되어
욕망의 사슬 끊어낸 고요

경내를 흔드는 타종 소리만
두물머리 흐름으로 울려 퍼진다.

Buddha's Birthday

So Yeong Seo

On the front yard of the Soojung Temple
The petals of the cherry tree fall drip drip
Laying the silk fabric
Greeting the worshippers

Who built the stone tower
Every stone placed with the weight of hope
Feels heavy on the gorgeous spring day

All those souls hanging lotus lanterns
Full of devotion
Lit lotus lanterns with various colors
The skein of karma of all existence
Of the universe
Passing through
A long tunnel of metempsychosis

Embracing the worthless desire
Contempted soul by possessing
Become an ascetic by strong will
Serenity
That cuts the chain of temptation

The sound of a bell shakes the temple
Echoing
Through the branches of the river.

[W's Magazine USA]

복수초여

서소영

겨우내내 기다림 하나로
호흡하며 살다
잔설 위에 수줍은 미소
바로 너였구나

가시덤불 속
멍울진 속살을 감추고
꽃으로 피워낸
노오란 빛깔이

아팠던 불면의 시간
지우고 지워도 지울 수 없었던
내 그리움을 닮았구나

다시 어둠에 묻히고
별빛 글썽이면
눈밭에 심장 얼어붙을
복수초여

피할 수 없는 인연
함께 가야 할 길이라면
하얀 밤 사랑이 젖도록
백치의 춤사위
어깨춤 추워보자.

Adonis Amurensis

So Yeong Seo

Winter long Just waiting
Lives to breathe
Shy smile on the snow
It is you

In the thornbush
Hides bruised flesh
Flower's blossom
Yellowish hue

Painful sleepless times
Attempt to erase repeatedly
However unerasable
Much like my yearning

Buried in the darkness again
As the starlight is moistened
As the heart freezes on a snowy field
Adonis Amurensis

Unavoidable fate
Must accompany on this road
The white night full of intimacy
Idiocy dance
Let's shoulder dance.

[NEW YORK-KOREA TIMES]

[Chance Encounter]

만남 하나로

김옥순

인연 되어 만나니 반갑고
멀리 있다 하여도 사랑함이라
풀잎 이슬 맞으며 밤을 기다리듯
이슬 먹고 피어나는 꽃이기에
그리움에 향기 묻어내며
노래하고 춤추리라
빈 가지 나무도 냉한설
겨울을 보내는 이유가 있듯이
어느 날 봄이 찾아와 푸른 옷 입혀
너울너울 춤을 추리라
이제는 더 이상 어디로
떠나지 않기를 바라는 마음
새싹이 꽃 피어 향기 젖는 날
그들은 함께 행복해 하리라.

Chance Encounter

Ok Soon Kim

Glad to meet because of karma
Loving even if far away
Like a glass leaf waits for night
While wetted with dew
For a flower swallows dew to bloom
Cover yearning with aroma
Shall dance while singing
Frosty winter even leafless tree
Like there's a reason
To let winter dissipate
One day spring returns to dress
With green cloth
Dancing fluttering–fluttering
No desire to leave anyplace anymore
Heart wishes not to leave
The day a bud blossoms a flower
Is drenched with aroma
They shall be happy together.

[ATLANTA–KOREA DAILY]

오페라의 유령

이경희

갑자기 추워진 날씨에
잔뜩 움츠려진 몸과 마음으로
동네를 어슬렁 거리다
책 대여점엘 들렀다

낡은 책들에서 풍기는 매캐함이 참 좋다
보물찾기에 열중인데
구석 후미진 곳에서
날 바라보는 번뜩이는 두 눈!
순간
난 심장이 오그라들 듯 한 전율을 느끼며 그에게 다가갔다
“오페라의 유령”

호기심 반... 기대 반

침침한 눈에 돋보기까지 동원하여
까만 밤이 하얗게 되도록
그 유령의 마력에 흠씬
그리곤
실로 오랜만에 느껴보는 벅찬 희열

불행한 삶을 살다간 주인공...유령 에릭
그의 연인...크리스틴 다에
그 여자의 연인...샤니 자작

유령의 처연한 사랑
비록
그것이 소설 속 허구의 사랑일망정
내 가슴을, 볼을 타고 흐르는 뜨거움
그것을 주체할 수가 없었다

슬프도록 가슴 시린 러브 스토리!

오늘 밤도
난
유령을 찾아 떠나야겠다.

The Phantom of the Opera

Gyeong Hi Lee

Strolling the village in the
Sudden cold weather
The man with shrinking body and soul
Stopped by a library

Aroma of the old books making me
Feel good
While searching for a treasure
Something stares fiercely at me
With glittering eyes
In a moment
Walking closer to him
While my heart started to flutter
"The Phantom of the Opera"

Prepare a pair of eye glasses
For deficient eyes

Until deep night turns to early dawn
Sucked into the spell of the phantom
It truly has been long
Since feeling this ecstati
How sadly miserable life was
Phantom Eric

His lover...Christine Daae
Her lover...Vicomte de Chagny

Phantom's wretched love
Even though
Just a fairy tale
I couldn't control
The flow of burning flame in my heart

Agonizingly heart-breaking love story!

Even tonight
I
Look for the phantom.

[CHICAGO-KOREA DAILY]

어이 여보시게

김수일

대 우주엔 태초란 있을 수가 없소
다만 무한으로 흐르는 시간이 있을 뿐이요
공허함으로 흘러가는 시간
지극함이 사랑이자 마음 곧 대 우주인 나요
그 마음이 하고 싶었던 일이 있었던 거요
그 일은 대 우주인 나의 표현이었고
표현은 현상으로 피워내는 생명이였소
제 각기 다른 현상으로 피워낸 생명들 말이오
그 생명들은 곧 나의 또 다른 모습이요
내 모습은 변화요
그 어느 것이라도 변화의 과정에 있소
끊임없이 생장소멸 하는 법칙 말이오
수초를 살다가는 원시 생명체도
빅뱅으로 피고 지는 저 넓은 우주도
똑같은 섭리로 오는 나의 마음이자 모습이오
당신은 볼 수 없는 저 세상도 대우주인 나
그래서 나는 알지만 당신은 모르오
당신은 현상계 끊임없이 변화하는 모습만
보고있을 뿐이요
대우주인 나는 변화이자 모든 현상이요
언제나 변화의 과정에 있는 진행형의 모습
늘 새롭게 천지를 창조
천지창조는
무한의 시간 속에 그 시간을 타고 흐른다오
어이 여보시게
아직도 모르겠소 나를 알아보겠소.

Hey

Soo Il Kim

In this universe
There is not the beginning of time
Exists only the time
That flows infinitely
Time flows meaninglessly
Faith is love and soul
Which is the universe that is me
That mind had a desire to do something
That was an expression of me
Who is the universe
The expression is a life
That blossoms into phenomenon
Lives that blossom into individually
Unique phenomenon
Those lives are other images of myself
My being is diversity
Everything is in the midst of transition
The endless rules of life and death
Primitive life form
That lives just a few seconds
That wide universe that blossomed
And scattered by the big bang
It's my image and soul alike destiny
Other side of the universe

Where you can not see also is me
So I know you don't
You only see
The endless transformations
The phenomenon and transformations
Is me who is the universe
Always in the progressive
Form to transition
The universe always changing
The birth of the universe is
Stream on the time of the infinite
Hey
Can't you tell it's me.

[CHICAGO-KOREA DAILY]

[Hey]

앞집 할아버지

모지선

이른 아침
논두렁 사이에 작은 나무이었다가
해 질 녘 산 아래
작은 그림자 되어
어느 순간 황톳빛 이랑으로 숨어 버린다

팔십도 훨씬 넘으신
호호백발 앞집 할아버지!
허리가 몹시 굽어
앉은키나 선키나 같으신 할아버지
언제나 땅만 보고 걸으신다

이 논에서 저 논으로
이 밭에서 저 밭으로
작은 짐승처럼 소리 없이 움직인다

외롭다거나 고독하다거나
그런 말들은
부질없는 내 마음
혼자 울먹이고
눈물짓는다

재작년 돌아가신 할머니는
뒷산에 묻으시고
모두가 떠나버린 텅 빈 낡은 집에서
어제도 그랬고
오늘도 그랬다

아침엔 논두렁 사이에 작은 나무였다가
해 질 녘 산 아래 작은 그림자 되어
어느 순간
황톳빛 이랑 사이로 사라져버린다.

The Grandpa Next Door

Ji Seon Mo

Early morning
Being a small tree between the levees
At the mountain bank at sunset
Become a small shadow
Hiding between the yellow fleshed furrows

Well over eighty years old
White haired next door grandpa!
He is bent at the waist badly
Grandpas heights sitting
And standing are the same
He walks always looking down

This rice field to that rice field
This field to that field
Quietly moving like a small animal

Lonely or solitary
Those words are
Useless my mind
Sobbing alone
Then shedding tears
Grandma passed away two years ago
Burried on the nearby hillside

In the house worn by time
Where everyone left
Yesterday and
Today remains the same

Early morning being a small tree
Between levees then
Become a small shadow
On the mountain bank
At sunset in a moment
Disappearing between
The yellow flashed furrows.

[CHICAGO-KOREA DAILY]

향수

양태영

어둠이 떠밀리고 벗겨지는
청옥 빛 하늘 멀리
고향 하늘엔 구름 글 벗기고

고개 숙인 이마에
지저귀는 새벽 별 하나
저 별은 !
오늘도 내게로 다가와

고향에 묵었던 바람을 들고서
나직한 목소리로 안녕을 고한다
우리 모두 잘 있음을
너도 또한 잘 있기를
지난밤 가슴에 발갛게 응어리지던 향수를

어느 누군가가 내게 준 고향에 향수
추억에 취하게 하고 나를 잠들게 한다.

Nostalgia

Tae Yeong Yang

Far away sky, sapphire aura
Chase and uncover the darkness
Uncover the cloud of the hometown

At the forehead of the bowed head
An early dawn's star is chattering
That star is!
Coming to me even today

Picking up the wind
That resides in the hometown
Whispering goodbye
We will be fine
Wishing you to remain well
Last night my heart was aching
With nostalgia

Somebody spurred
My memories of the hometown
Got me intoxicated with those memories
Then put me to sleep.

[CHICAGO-KOREA DAILY]

저녁노을

조금주

저 붉은 노을은
고요한 겨울 바다에서
숨죽여 가며 내 혈관을 타고
흐르는 빨간 눈시울이다

두둥실 떠다니는
하얀 구름에
붉은 열정으로 물들이며
길 잃은 양떼들이 몰려온다

저녁노을은
손닿을 듯 말듯
여기저기 떠돌다가
세찬 칼바람을 멈추고
붉게 타오르는 정열이다.

Evening Twilight

Geum Ju Jo

That reddish twilight
At the calm winter ocean moves
Breathlessly through my blood vessels
Streams of reddish eyerims

Floating in the air
On a cloud
Dyed with reddish passion
A herd of sheep is coming

Evening twillight
Could be reached or not
Wandering around
Stop the gusting wind
Reddish burning passion.

[NEW YORK-KOREA TIMES]

[Evening Twilight]

[Rainy Day]

비오는 날

조금주

하늘에서
슬픈 울음소리 들리면
날 창가에 세우게 하고
고개를 떨구게 한다

사랑을 고이 담아
추억을 스쳐 지나게 하고
타오르는 마음 곱게 접어
널 보낸 후에 멈추게 한다

떨어지는 빗방울은
땅에 부딪히는 난타음악
우렁차게 파도 치는 마음속에
고요함을 살그머니 훔쳐온다.

Rainy Day

Geum Ju Jo

From the sky
Hear the sound of sad crying
Makes me stand next to the window
And lower my head

Gather the love carefully
Let the past memory fade
Fold over burning desire nicely
Stopping after allowing your leave

Raindrops falling down
Making music on the ground
Roaring waving in the heart
Steal the silence stealthly.

[CHICAGO-KOREA DAILY]

숨비소리

전기예

흐트러진 세월
얼마나 파도를 삼키어 토해냈을까

주상 전리대의 모양새는
까맣게 타버린 그녀들이
반듯하게 깎아 다듬어낸 세월일까

태왁이 던져질 때마다
출렁대는 물결에 실어
뭍으로 보낸 어린 얼굴

웃음 가득 담아
물 위에 떠오르는
숨비소리 세상에 퍼지면

눈가의 주름
고향길 돌담 모퉁이를
바람을 타고 와
문고리 머무는
애환의 손짓

밤이 지나면
또 다시 태왁을 던지며
수면을 가득 채울 숨비소리는
그들만의 수궁가.

The Deep Breath of the Female Diver

Ki Ye Jeon

Scattered past memories
Mouth open, swallow and throw up the waves

Joosang's columnar basalt looks like
Chiseled, shaped
And straightened past memories
By women divers
Who got burned pitch black

Every time the trap's buoy is thrown
Young face is sent to the shore
On the undulating waves

Road of smiles
Surface on the sea
Reverberate the deep breath
Of the female diver

Wrinkled eyes
Around the edge of the stone wall
Of the hometown
Ride on the wind
Stay at the door handle
Waving of happiness and sorrow

When the night is gone
Throw the trap's buoy again
Then the deep breath
Of the female divers is
Their music.

[NEW YORK-KOREA TIMES]

[The Deep Breath of the Female Diver]

작달비

전기예

너울대는 욕망의 환상이
너로 인해 깨어져도 원망보다는
감사하는 위선으로 너를 바라보련다

세상을 아름답게 꾸며내도
가슴 속으로 더 깊게 져며 드는 욕심에
너마저 피하고 싶어 처마밑에 숨은 아주 볼품없는 모양새다

아무도 없는 곳에 둥지 틀고
어쩌다 혼자 떠다니는 구름이라도 보면
쓴웃음도 한번 해보고
오늘같이 너를 만나면 다시 또 넋을 잃고

그래도 오늘이 지나가면 너를 또 기다린다
모두가 씻기어 흔적없이 사라져 훨훨 날아갈 수 있도록.

Pouring Rain

Ki Ye Jeon

Even if a fluttering illusion of passion
Is shattered by you
Stand by you with hypocrisy of gratitude
Ather than grievance

Even embellished
In the picturesque world
Desire to soak deep into the heart
Hide under the eaves to try to dodge
Even you
It is so absurd

Built a nest of solitude
If I see a wandering cloud
Once in a while
Make a brighter smile
If I meet you like today
After losing my mind

l shall wait for you even after today
Everything is cleaned then disappears
Without a trace
Fly away fluttering.

[CHICAGO-KOREA DAILY]

눈밭에 서서

임종은

소복소복
흰 눈이 내린다
나는 빈 들판에 갇혀
공포에 질린 토끼처럼
가쁜 숨을 몰아쉬며
눈을 맞고 있다

꽁꽁 언 하늘은
天地 간 널브러진
거짓과 위선에 포장된
추악한 온갖 허물을
통째로 덮으려는 듯
경건한 눈 洗禮(세례)를 내리고 있다

찬바람에 구르던 낙엽도
서서히 짓눌리는 위압감에
숨죽이고
樹液(수액) 운반하던 참나무 가지들도
하얀 무게를 보듬고 침묵하는데

누가 백색의 심판을
거역할 수 있는가?
산과 들
나무와 바위

모두가 순백의 聖域에 갇혀
懺悔(참회)에 떨고 있는데

아직도 나는
오염된 心性을 털어내지 못하고
흰 눈 무더기에 묻히고 있다
저렇듯 순수가 충만한 儀式에
동참하지 못한 체.

Standing on a Snowfield

Jong Eun Im

Aggregating cornucopia
White snow is coming down
I am restrained in a solitude field
Like a terrified rabbit
Breathing uneasily
Receiving the snowflakes

Frozen sky
Spread out world wide
Wrapped with deceit and hypocricy
All kinds of ugly negligence
Effort to cover entirely
Holy snowy blessing is coming down

Tumbling leaves by the torrent wind
Slow pressure
Holding breath
Branches of oak trees
That carries the sap
Embrace the white weight silently

Who dares to contradict the white judgement
Mountains and fields
Trees and rocks
The entire world is imprisoned
In a sanctuary of pure white
Tremble with repentance

Still I
Could not shake off the poisoned soul
That is buried under
The large accumulation of white snow
Could not be involved in
The ritual of abundance of innocense.

[CHICAGO-KOREA DAILY]

[Pouring Rain]

[Marching in the Midsummer]

한 여름의 행진

임종은

저 맞은편 함석지붕 위로
찬연히 빛나 부서지던 햇살이
잿빛 도로 위에 샅샅이 흩어지면

무기력한 의식은
낯익은 사하라 사막의
오아시스 변두리 서성거리며
권태를 되씹고

멀리 아득한 곳으로부터
증폭되어 밀려오는 긴 행렬의 굉음에
깜짝 놀란 도시의 심장은
더욱 가열되고

또 맹렬히 이글거리며
땅과 가까워지려는 태양은
노출의 장막을 하나씩 걷어내고
선글라스 가득히
농익은 여름을 담아
한여름을 행진하고 있다.

Marching in the Midsummer

Jong Eun Im

On the other side of the street
On the tin roof
Dazzling
Bright sunlight breaking apart
Scattering all over the soot–colored road

Powerless consciousness is
Walking around
The outskirt of the familiar
Sahara Desert's oasis
While chewing the boredom repeatedly

From afar
A long parade of amplified
Swarming, roaring sound
Surprising the heart of the city
Heating hotter

Again blazing brilliantly
Sun that wants to get closer
Takes off the curtain of exposure
Fill the sunglass
With overripe summer
Marching in the midsummer.

[NEW YORK–KOREA TIMES]

겨울편지

이우창

겨울 하늘에 눈이 덮여 있습니다
앞을 보지 못하게 내가 서 있습니다
아무도 돌아보지 않는 공간에 있습니다
내가 물어도 대답할 사람이 없습니다
긴 밤을 넓은 허공에 써야 합니다
혼자서 별을 찾아야 합니다
아직 해를 모르는 별이 있기에
별만큼 많이 겨울 편지를 씁니다
다시 보리라는 소망이 있기에
단 한 번의 사연에 추신을 붙입니다
이번엔 꼭 만납니다 하고
거부 할 수 없는 웃음을 보냅니다
마지막 겨울이 가기 전 답이 오기를
오늘처럼 비가 오면 다 눈이 녹아
나의 편지도 풀어질지 모릅니다
비가 가기 전에 어서 답을 주세요
혼자만의 그리움으로
이렇게 길게 써보는 것입니다.

Winter Letter

Woo Chang Lee

Winter sky is covered with snow
The view blocked by me
There is an abandoned space
Even if asked, there's nobody to answer
Need to write about long nights
On wide spaces
Searching for stars alone
There's stars that do not know
The existence of the sun
Writing the winter letters
As much as the stars
Because there is a hope
That we will meet again
Sending a P.S. just for a glance
From you
Writing "We must meet again this time"
Sending laughter you can not refuse
Hope you answer me
Before the end of the winter
If it rains like today
The snow shall melt away
Taking my letter with it
Please, answer me the rain is leaving
Writing long like this
As loneliness exists.

[CHICAGO-KOREA DAILY]

[Winter Letter]

할머니의 어린시절

정정채

할머니도 어린 시절이 있었느냐고 묻는
손녀의 초롱초롱한 눈빛 속에 까마득한
옛날 잊었던 추억이 주마등처럼 스친다

바람, 그리고 꽃과 나비로
오색 커튼 둘러치고 파란
구름으로 멍석 만들고

모래알로 밥해 놓고 깻잎
호박잎 나물 무쳐 사금파리
소반 위에 휘영청 차려놓고
동네 꼬마 불러 신랑 각시
놀이하던 유년의 나날

너울너울 안개 면류관 쓰고
앵두 목걸이에 꽃반지 끼고
소달구지 가마에 올라앉아

고사리 손잡고 티 없이 웃던 시절
할머니 어린 시절을 묻는 어여쁜
손녀의 눈 속에 그때의 내가 있다.

Grandma's Childhood

Jeong Chae Jeong

Asking grandma if she ever had a childhood
In the granddaughter's twinkling eyes
Forgotten memories long past are
Like a revolving lantern

Wind, flower, and butterfly
Surrounded with brightly colored draperies
Make a straw carpet with the blue cloud

Cooking rice with sand
With leaves of sesame and pumpkin
Making salad on a broken plate
Preparing big dinner on a tray
Playing bride and groom
Good old childhood days

Wear the fluffy crown of mist
Cherry necklace and flower ring
Sitting on a cow carriage

Holding tiny hands
Those innocent happy days
Those days are in the cute
Granddaughter's eyes
Who's asking about
Grandma's childhood.

[W's Magazine USA]

봄

박인숙

냉이 다듬는 아낙의
뭉툭한 손끝에서

노릇노릇 익어가는
개나리 넝쿨 길 따라

진달래 한 아름
산 마루 고개 넘어

나풀한 바람 입고
봄이 찾아옵니다.

Spring

In Sook Park

From the blunt finger tips of a woman
Who trims Capsella bursapastoris

Following the road of
Golden ripe forsythia

An armful of Azalea
Over the ridge of the mountain

Spring comes
Wearing the fluttering wind.

[CHICAGO-KOREA DAILY]

[Spring]

[What Should We Do]

어쩌란 말입니까

박인숙

일 급수 물이
스스로 부정타 채찍질 하시면
어쩌란 말입니까

이 급수 삼 급수 물은
석고대죄도 모자랄 판
목을 맬 수도 없는 일
어쩌란 말입니까

말빚, 글빚에 파산 되어
어줍잖게 토해내는
속 찌꺼기들을
어쩌란 말입니까

무소유도 소유라
그림자 묻어 두고
그렇게 가십니다
어쩌란 말입니까.

What Should We Do

In Sook Park

Whipping because
First grade water is cursed by itself
What should we do

Second and third grade water is
Not enough to ask for mercy
Or hang by the neck on the rope
What should we do

Word debt, letter debt are bankruptcy
Ridiculously vomiting up
The guts' residue
What should we do

Burying the shadow
Because nonpossession is possession
You left like this
What should we do.

[NEW YORK–KOREA TIMES]

장날 오후

유영준

축 처진 어깨처럼
세월 속에 늙어 버린
늦가을 시골 거리
지나가는 서글픈 바람이
오늘따라 가래 끓는 소리를 낸다

이젠 서는 둥 마는 둥
너무 빨리 다가오기만 하는데
붐비려다 그냥 흩어져 버리는 장날
전(廛) 거두는 사람들의 발걸음만 분주한
허기진 오후

시골 장터 비좁은 길을
소달구지 하나가
삐걱거리며 돌아 나간다

싣고 가는 낡은 삽자루 뭉치에
젖은 회한(悔恨)이 배이면
채찍 잡은 주름진 손엔
땀방울마저 말라 버린다

저 멀리 논두렁길 너머로 마을이 보이고
밥 짓는 굴뚝마다 피어오르는 연기들이
저마다 정답게 고개를 내민다

길 따라 흩어진 낙엽들은
몸부림치다 진(津)이 빠져
그만 몸살이 나고 마는데

비스듬히 기댄 촌로의 겨드랑이 사이로
석양에 비친 그림자 하나가
길게 멀어져 가다 걸음을 멈춘다.

Farmer's Market in the Afternoon

Yeong Jun Yu

Like slouching shoulders
Growing older in time
Village street in late autumn
Today the passing lonely wind is making
A sound of obstructive phlegm
In the throat

Now hastily
Time comes so fast for the market day
Looks like there is a crowd but then they scatter
Just people's foot steps are busy to beat
The breaking down of tents
Exhausted afternoon

In the farmers market's narrow road
A cow carriage is
Going back home
While making creaking sounds

Carrying a bundle of worn shovels
That are soaked with wetting remorse
On the wrinkled hand that holds a whip
Sweat drops are dried

The village can be seen
Over the footpath of the rice field
Every rice cooking chimney
With smoke arising
Saying hello nicely

On the road fallen scattered leaves are
Writhing then resin seeps out then
Gets sick with fatigue

Seen between
The armpit of a leaning village elder
A reflected shadow on the sunset
After drifting long the foot steps cease.

[CHICAGO-KOREA DAILY]

꽃구경(꽃상여)
-장사익 명창의 노래 중에서

세상 꽃 천지 어느 봄날
꽃구경 가자는 아들의 등에 얼싸 업혀

마을 지나 개울 건너 산허리 질러 숲은 짙어지고
이상타 놀란 어머니 어이쿠, 고려장 치를 황천길일세!

내 새끼 등에 마지막으로 업혀가니
억울타 말 못하고 밤 낯선 산길 아래
아들마저 잃을까 솔잎 따서 길 이으시며

아들아 아들아 천금같은 내 아들아
내 몸은 갈 날이지만
금지옥엽 니몸 어디 다칠랑가

뿌려진 솔 뭉치 따라
조근조근 잘 살펴 가려무나

장사익 소리꾼의 꽃구경처럼
늙고 병든 부모님을 마음에서 버린 적은 없었는지

버린 듯이 잊고 산 것은 아니었나
홀로 계신 내 어머니 생각으로 가슴이 따가워 옵니다.

글 : 한신디아

Strolling

song by Sa Ik Jang

Mother let's go strolling
Hop on my back
Let's go strolling

On a spring day
The whole world is full of flower blossoms
Mother happily hops on son's back
Through the village and through the field
On the mountain road
Swelled thick with trees
My God mother was speechless

Spring stroll flower stroll close the eyes
Handful handful pick pine needles
While strolling
Scatter them on the returning roads

Mother what are you doing
What are you doing
Why are you not strolling
Why are you scatter the pine needles

Son son my son
I'm worried that you have gone back
On this road alone
I'm worried that you will be wandering
Lost on these mountain roads.

[CHICAGO–KOREA DAILY]

[장사익 명창의 글씨]

백두여, 하늘연못이여!

박종규

천지 가득
민족의 하늘 담고
태초부터 반도에 웅자 틀어
세세토록 한 얼이 되어 준
백두白頭

장엄하다, 장엄하다!

오천 년 세월 빗금 진 돌계단 위
살 차게 우주로 열린 네 위용
천기 서린 물빛에 보석이 된
하늘 연못
벅찬 가슴 풀어
여기 설렘의 눈물 뿌린다

골 안개도 비 무리도 벗개고
청수정 해안解顔 햇살 가득한
천지는
마르고 갈라진 한恨 동여맬 혼으로
정기 씻고 채워 둔 민족의 혈
하늘빛 이룬 성지

천지여,
나 이제 너를 두고 떠나나
금 간 역사의 비문碑文 바로 서는 날까지
또 다른 나는 백골 한뉘토록
천지에 천추千秋로 남고 싶어라.

[사진제공 / 박종규]

Baekdoo and Chunji !

Chong Kyu Park

Filled in Lake Chunji
With ancestor's heaven
Bear the gallant one on the penninsula
Since the beginning of the world
Become a unique spirit generation after generation
Mt. Baekdoo

Grandiose, Grandiose!

Stone staircase that eroded for five thousand years
Your massive majestic
Being opening up to the universe
Becomes a jewel that's covered by heavenly force with sparkling water
Heavenly lake
Open the heart with overwhelming feelings
Accompanied by fluttering eyedrops

Remove the valley mist and rain cloud
Fill it with coastal blue crystal sunlight
Lake Chunji
Mend and cleanse the dried and cracked soul
With our ancestor's blood and aura
Holy land that was built with heavenly radiance

Lake Chunji,
Now sadly I am leaving you
Until the day that this epitaph of broken history stands righteous
Along with the ashes of the spirit's bones the heart
Desires to remain at Lake Chunji for a thousand years.

[NEW YORK-KOREA TIMES]

그리하리라

박종규

하늘 바다
그 넓은 가슴에 빠져
쉽도록 소리치고 싶다
쩌엉 쩌엉 하늘 가르는
외침 하나로
그대 곁에 가고 싶노라고

그대 깊음 깊고 깊어
태산 아래 골짜기라도
하늘 가득 담긴 그 담소에 빠져
나 영영 수장되고 말지라도
그대 사랑 거기 있음에

처음부터 수평으로 하나였던 우리
다시는,
다시는 바람이 나누지 못하도록
두 손 길게 늘려 동여매리라
눈빛 눈빛으로 일군 불꽃 타올라
하늘 바다 다 말리도록.

Do So

Chong Kyu Park

Ocean sky
Falling into the spacious heart
Desires to scream sadly
Whoosh whoosh across the sky
With a shout
Wishes to be close to you

Your depth is unfathomable
The valley under Mountain Tae
Obliged to fall into the reservoir engulfing the sky
Even if buried in the water forever

We are harmoniously together since the beginning of time
Never,
Ever again divided by the wind
Embracing with long stetched arms
Burning flame ignited by the glitter of the eye
Ocean sky until completely dry.

[ATLANTA-KOREA DAILY]

[Do So]

[Being in Love]

사랑하고 있음이

김용복

그 사람이 어디가 좋으냐고 묻습니다
그냥 좋다고 말합니다
다른 사람은 겉만 보고 말하지만
내가 보는 그는 마음씨가 아름답습니다

그 사람을 사랑하느냐고 묻습니다
사랑하기에 좋아한다고 말합니다
다른 사람은 겉만 보고 묻지만
나는 바라만 보아도 설레 입니다

그 사람 언제부터 좋아했나를 묻습니다
처음 보는 순간이라 말합니다
어떻게 그리되느냐 말하지만
이미 내 가슴에 있음이 느껴집니다

그 사람 언제부터 사랑했나를 묻습니다
처음 보는 순간이라 답합니다
어떻게 그리 사랑하느냐 말하지만
그녀가 나를 사랑하고 있음이 느껴집니다.

Being in Love

Yong Bok Kim

Asking me why am I in love
Say I am in love without reason
Others in love with look of love
I am in love because of his heart

Asking me am I in love with her
Say I like it because I am in love
Others asking questions because they don't like looks
But I am in love with everything about her

Asking me since when have I been in love
Tell them I was in love the very first time I saw her
Asking me how can I be
I already feel she is in my heart

Asking me since when have I been in love
Tell them I was in love the very first time I saw her
Asking me how can I be deeply in love
I feel that she is in love with me.

[NEW YORK-KOREA TIMES]

편지

김용복

노을지는 해변에서
조각조각 부서지는
파도 속의 거품을 바라보며
흩어진 추억의 조각을 맞춰보는
퍼즐게임에 빠져 있소

화선지에 퍼지는 먹물처럼
파도 따라 밀려오는 추억들
머릿속에 남은 당신 모습을 맞춰보지만
물안개 속의 피사체처럼
희미한 잔상만 스케치하오

천 년을 약속한 사랑도
백 년도 못되어 상실로 묻히고
가슴에 느낌을
손끝에 잡아보지만
바람만이 가슴에 구멍을 냈소

부질없는 일이라
몇 수번 다짐을 해 보지만
그래도 가슴 한구석에 남는 미련
수취인 없는 낙조에 걸어
편지를 띄웁니다.

Letter

Yong Bok Kim

On the beach at sunset
Looking in the wave's bubbles
Breaking into a thousand pieces
Making a puzzle game
Putting together
The scattered pieces of memories

Like ink dispersing on a paper
Surging memories following the wave
Attach the pieces of memories
Of you together
Like a subject in the mist
Drawing the blurry vestige

Even the devoted love
For a thousand years
Buried by forfeiture less
Than a hundred years
Feelings in the heart
Beholden with finger tips
The wind makes a hole in the heart

Pledging many times
That is useless desire
But lingering attachment remains
A remote part of my heart
On ebb tides with no recipient
Send a letter.

[CHICAGO-KOREA DAILY]

[Letter]

[Seogwipo]

서귀포에서

김인수

서귀포 해안을 따라
줄지어 선 이국 아이들
색이 다른 모습으로 어깨동무를 한다

이름도 성도 서로 달라
인사도 알아듣지 못하나
서로 웃으며 서 있는 모습이 대견하다

서귀포 70리
병풍처럼 둘러진 모습에
자연의 성스러움을 본다

작은 점으로 오랫동안 서서
취해있는 나와
스스로 친구가 되어 주는
서귀포 해안 뒤로
햇살을 수줍어하며
붉어진
바다의 얼굴은 홍안이다.

Seogwipo

In Soo Kim

On the Seogwipo coastline
Kids from out of this world
Stand on a line
Distinguished colored
Shoulder to shoulder

Everyone has a unique name
Could not communicate
Smiling at each other
Looking mighty fine

Twenty miles of Seogwipo
Looks like a mural painting
Nature's divine view

Standing a long time as a tiny point
I am under its spell
Become friends naturally
Behind the Seogwipo coast
Shy for sunlight
Reddish
The face of the ocean is a rosy cheek.

[CHICAGO-KOREA DAILY]

어머니

김블라시오

언제나 불러도 불러도
정겹고 그리운 이름이여

그 곱디고운 손마디는
자식들의 뒷바라지로 헤어지고

그 아름답던 얼굴은
어느새 주름살로 흠뻑 패이고

등굽은 허리는 세월의 무상함
아는가 모르는가 모정의 마음을.

Mother

Blasio Kim

When calling and calling
The yearning of that tender name

Those soft and gentle fingers
Roughed from caring for children

That beautiful face
Now bombarded with wrinkles

The bent back is unconscious of time
Is there awareness
Or not of a loving mother's heart.

[CHICAGO-KOREA DAILY]

영원한 섬, 독도
-독도는 말한다

김블라시오

우리가 지켜야 할 하늘과 땅 그리고 바다
오늘도 동도가 말하고 서도가 외친다
나를 지켜 달라고 그리고 알아 달라고
새들과 별들의 고향 우리의 낙원

600년 전 우산도란 이름으로
세종실록지리지에 등재된 우리의 땅
왕해국은 알고 있다
강치도 알고 있다

말없이 지켜보는 저 등대와
괭이갈매기와 슴새도 보고 있다
아름다운 동방의 나라
대한민국의 위대한 섬 독도라고

탕건봉과 삼형제굴 바위의 전설이 담긴
세계를 향해 나아갈 한민족의 땅이 노래한다
독도를 지키고 알아달라고
오늘도 서로 사랑하면서 용서하라고.

Eternal Island, Dokdo
Subtitle: Dokdo Speaks

Blasio Kim

The sky, land and ocean that we must protect
Dongdo is speaking
And Suhdo is shouting again today
Protect me and know me
The birthplace of birds
And stars are our paradise

Usando was named 600 years ago
Our land that was mapped
During the Seijong Dynasty
Aster flowers know it
And sea lions know it

Along with the lighthouse
That oversees in silence
The Black-tailed gull
And shearwaters are watching
The magnificent eastern country
A wonderful island of Korea called Dokdo

This place from folk tales
A land of Korea that is standing tall
And proud is facing
The world and singing
Protect and know Dokdo
Love and forgive each other even today.

[NEW YORK-KOREA TIMES]

사랑

조선미

사랑
사랑이 뭔지 아직 모르겠어요

그대를 생각하면
가슴이 두근두근
짜릿한 감정
그립고 기다려지는 이 마음
이런 것이 사랑인가요

솜털처럼 흐르는 구름이
님 오시는 것 같아
가슴 졸이며 마중하는 이 마음
이런 것이 사랑인가요

사랑
사랑이 뭔지 아직 모르겠어요.

Love

Seon Mi Jo

Love
I don't know what love is yet

When I think of you
My heart beats faster
I get this thrilling sensation
Missing and yearning for you
Could this be love

These clouds
That flow like cotton feathers
Makes me feel like my lover is coming
My heart tightens with eager anticipation
Could this be love

Love
I don't know what love is yet.

[CHICAGO-KOREA DAILY]

[Love]

[Because You're Coming]

네가 온다고 하니

한승석

네가 온다고 하니 하늘도 반가 와서
천지는 순백의 물결로 출렁이고
길섶마다 흰 눈송이
소복이 단장하고 있구나

황량한 여기 시골 논 한가운데
흰 두루미 한 쌍이 날개짓하며
하늘 높이 날아오르는구나

천 리 길 머나먼 길을 오는 친구야
산 넘고 강 건너 험한 준령을 돌아
이곳에 오기까지 얼마나 힘들 까나

가슴으로 말하는 친구야
우리 함께 희망을 이야기 나누며
그리움의 저편에서 만나자꾸나.

Because You're Coming

Seung Seok Han

Because you're coming, even the sky is pleased
Waiving the crystal clear water of Lake Chunji
Feathery snowflakes
Covering the area

In the middle of the destitute countryside
A pair of white cranes are flapping
Their wings high up in the sky

Friend coming from thousands of miles away
Around the rough mountain and crossing the river
How hard it is to travel here

Friend talking with warm heart
Speaking of our destiny together
Let us rendezvous on the other side of yearning.

[NEW YORK-KOREA TIMES]

가난한 사람

천도화

나는 당신에게
가난한 사람입니다

사랑 때문에 울어야 하는
가난한 사람입니다

잠을 자거나
길을 걷거나
일을 하거나
내 걸음은 오직 하나
당신 앞에서는
가난한 사람입니다

빈 가슴에
심어준 사랑의 싹
꽃피워 향기나는
내 마음은 당신 앞에
가난한 사람입니다.

Hopeless One

Cheon Do Hwa

I am to you
Hopeless one

Crying for love
I am a hopeless one

While asleep
While walking
While working
My step is only one
In front of you
I am a hopeless one

In the empty heart
Plant a sprout of love
Blossom to aroma
In front of you
My mind is a hopeless one.

[NEW YORK-KOREA TIMES]

[Hopeless One]

[The Wind Cries in Hiding]

숨어우는 바람

천도화

그대 그리운 날에는
꽃비가 내리고
그대 보고픈 날에는
장미 향기가 났지

봄은 여름으로 떠나고
상처 난 가슴은
몸살을 하는데

잠을 자도 눈을 떠도
그리운데
그리운데
난들 어쩌겠소.

The Wind Cries in Hiding

Cheon Do Hwa

While yearning for you
It rains flowers
While missing you
The aroma of roses rises

Spring leaves to summer
The broken heart is
Shivering

While asleep while awake
Yearning
Yearning
What should I do.

[CHICAGO-KOREA DAILY]

선인장

이길옥

가끔
내부 깊숙이 웅크린 불만을 뽑아들고 있었다
그때마다
불길 같은 비늘을 떨구며 일어서는 야생의 눈으로
동해의 바다가 마르는 것을 보고 있었다
하늘로 솟는 기염(氣焰)도 보고 있었다
더러는 허리를 접히면서도
정물이 되어 화폭에 갈아 앉으면서도
그대의 잃어버린 고향을 노래하며
서럽게 웃어 보일 꽃이라도 피웠었다
아픈 세월을 뿌리에 감아
모래알 사이를 비집고 들면서도
물기를 만난 웃음 때문에
잎은 가시로 돋고
살점 부서진 자리에도
생명의 눈은 진득거리고 있었다
오한과 갈증의 사태에 깔려
시장기의 회오리에 몰리면서도
눈에 보이지 않는 몸부림 한 번으로
이국의 창변에서 가시로 웃고 있었다.

The Cactus

Gil Ok Lee

Sometime
Pull out the disenchanted
That crouches deep inside
At times
With wild eyes that stand up
While shaking off the scales
Like a blaze
Looking at the East Sea to dry
Looking at the high spirit rising up
To the sky
Bent over at the waist once in a while
Singing for your forgotten hometown
A flower blossoms
Even though it looks like sad laughter
Wind painful times up around the root
Rooting
Between the gaps of the sand grains
Even though the smile meets the moisture
So leaves arise as thorns
Where the flesh broke off
Life's eye is viscous
Buried by a landslide of rigor and thirst
As bitten by the cyclone of starving
Invisible squirming one time
Laughing as a thorn
At the window of an alien land.

[CHICAGO-KOREA DAILY]

[The Cactus]

[Someone Who Loves Me]

나를 사랑하는 사람은

이길옥

먼 데서
희미하게 들리는
목소리만으로도 나를 안다

소리 죽여 걷는
발소리만으로도 알고

가늘게 흔들리는
뒷모습만으로도 나를 안다

눈빛만으로
내 깊은 속마음을 알고

얼굴만 보고도
내 깊은 속 뜻을 안다

나를
사랑하는 사람은.

Someone Who Loves Me

Gil Ok Lee

From a distance
The whispering of
My voice recognizes me

Even when I walk like a cat
It notices me

Standing far away
Glancing me from behind it identifies me

Through the glare of my eyes
Can read my deep thoughts

Gaze into my face
Can understand my inner feelings

Someone
Who loves me.

[NEW YORK-KOREA TIMES]

통일

김정덕

반만년 역사 위에 빛나는 우리 전통
화려한 금수강산 지켜온 우리 국가

신라의 화랑정신 삼국통일 이룩했고
위나라 오촉멸해 새역사 바꾸었네

삼일의 만세 소리 한반도에 떨쳤었고
중국의 五.四운동 천하를 뒤덮었네

운명의 같은 핏줄 나뉘어진 우리 동포
피맺힌 포성 소리 천하를 물들였네

五.一六 군사혁명 난국을 구제했고
중국의 신해혁명 중화민국 이룩했네

과거를 거울삼아 미래를 내다보면
우리의 평화통일 총화에서 비롯되네.

A Wish for Unification of Korea

Jeong Deok Kim

We have cherished a brilliant tradition
Based upon a great long history

Our ancestors owed the reunification of three tribal nations
To the Wha-Rang Spirit during the Sinla Dynasty

The lingering sound of the March Anti-Japanese rally
Seems to still spread all over the country

Sorrowful separation of the brethren is now suffered
In the wake of the cannons' roar from the North

Backed by the honorable fathers' bravery
Instead we shall attain total security from peaceful unity.

[NEW YORK-KOREA TIMES]

[A Wish for Unification of Korea]

SOFT
SHOULDER

어느날 그대가 다시 찾아오리

김정덕

좋은 꽃은 항상 피어 있지 아니하고
좋은 경치는 항상 존재하지 아니하네

이별의 근심 쌓여 눈언저리 미소를 풀고
눈물이 술잔에 지어 상봉할 것을 기약하네

이 술잔 비우고
안주 좀 드사이다

인생이 몇 번 취하기 어려우니
또다시 마시기를 고대하기 기껍잖으니
자! 한 잔 드사이다

오늘 밤 이별 후
어느 날 그대가 다시 찾아오리.

When Do You Come Back Again

Jeong Deok Kim

Exotic flower of the perennial type
Majestic scenery does not exist for eternity

Enormous anxiety of seperation dissipates
The smile around the eye

Eyedrops fill a wine glass to promise dejavu
Bottoms up
Have some appetizers

Life is hard feeling intoxicated many times
Let's cheers
As I can hardly wait to drink again

After tonight's departure
Someday we shall meet again.

[ATLANTA-KOREA DAILY]

귀천

천상병

나 하늘로 돌아가리라
새벽빛 와 닿으면 스러지는 이슬
더불어 손에 손을 잡고

나 하늘로 돌아가리라
노을빛 함께 단둘이서
기슭에서 놀다가 구름 손짓하며는

나 하늘로 돌아가리라.
아름다운 이 세상 소풍 끝내는 날
가서, 아름다웠더라고 말하리라.

Going Back to Heaven

Sang Byeong Cheon

I am going back to heaven
The dew drop that evaporates with the touch of the dawn light
Together ascend hand in hand

I am going back to heaven
With the twilight togather just the two of us
Playing near the base of the mountain until the cloud waves at us

I am going back to heaven
At the end of the picnic of the beautiful world
Upon arrival I shall tell how beautiful it was.

[ATLANTA-KOREA DAILY]

[When Do You Come Back Again]

[How to Live Alone]

How to Live Alone

Gil Jae

If gusting cyclone is not blowing
A chapel of silent prayer where I lay alone
The moon light brightens the entire village
Delight in the stroll alone

Rain flows endlessly at the end of the eaves
Dreaming of the sky with the pillow at times raised higher
When snow falls all over the mountain
With the tea's aroma living without anxiety.

사나운 회오리바람 불어오지 않으니
홀로 누운 단칸방도 고요의 선방(禪房)이며
밝은 달도 초야에 가득 드리워지니
홀로 거니는 발걸음도 가볍구나

처마 끝에 빗물이 계속 흐르면
이따금 베개를 높이 하여 하늘 꿈을 꾸고
산중에 눈이 펄펄 날리면
다향(茶香)에 시름 놓고 사는구나.

이 시는 길창근(긴뚝 섬)님의 선조이신 야은 길재선생이 유배지에서 외로움으로 만드신 시조를 현대 시감으로 풀이 한 아름다운 글입니다.

[Hope-wind/배달래 화가] [A Prayer for You]
Painting on Body & mixed media on Canvas / 162×102cm / 2009

A Prayer for You

Cynthia Han

Melancholy

At the intensely absolute moment of solitude
Like the far away church bell's ring
Filled with low tones that linger and reflect

In the frosty winter
Feel the naked tree's soundless texture of the breathing
Over the dawn with a prayer for you

Like Lycoris squamigera that constantly misses each other
Our rendezvous gradually to ebb
Like young wave's hesitation

Toward the ocean salted with yearning
Endlessly
Promises with our aspirations

For you I shall be
The silent wave
Devastated by loneliness and then solely disintegrated.

[SEOUL-KOREA LITERATURE NEWSPAPER]

[Healing of the Soul]

Healing of the Soul

Cynthia Han

Companionless, empty heart
With friendship, let the isolation be healed

Loveless, broken heart
With the song of a poet, let the confinement be healed

Spiritless, abandoned universe
With God's blessing, let the death be healed

Lifelessness, fogotten name
With a star's lucidness, let the soul be healed.

[ATLANTA-KOREA DAILY]

「Sense of Aroma」 제1집을 발간하면서...

「Sense of Aroma」 제1집이 탄생하기까지 한신디아 시인과 윤요안 사진작가 그리고 많은 시인들의 적극적인 참여와 열의로 이제 빛나는 영광의 결실을 보게 되었습니다.

나라사랑, 한글사랑이라는 애국심을 가슴에 달고 우리문학을 국외에 널리 알리겠다는 하나 된 이념 아래 서양지천으로 우리글이 널리 퍼져 있을 그날까지 이번 한·영번역시집의 주인공이 되었다는 사실 하나만으로도 참여 시인들의 자부심은 큰 감동이 아닐 수가 없습니다.

앞으로도 (사)대한민국국보문학협회에서는 문학창작 활동의 가장 앞서가는 세계적인 안목을 꾸준히 지원할 것이며, 모든 문학창작인들의 다양한 활동을 적극 후원 할 것임을 약속드립니다.

이 책 「Sense of Aroma」가 대한민국 문단의 절대 숙원인 노벨문학상 수상을 꿈꾸는 디딤돌이 되기를 간절히 희망하여 봅니다.

여러분, 진심으로 감사드립니다!

2010년 4월

발행인 **임수홍**